What's Up With You, Taquandra Fu?

written by Matt Cibula
illustrated by Brian Strassburg

Zino Press
CHILDREN'S BOOKS

Madison, Wisconsin

This book is dedicated to all the kids who wrote to the Contrary Kid, and to the great Emma Simone Cibula, who makes Taquandra seem like Normal McNormal
—M.C.

To Carl and Ruth—B.S.

What's Up With You, Taquandra Fu? is proudly published by Zino Press Children's Books, P.O. Box 52, Madison, WI 53701. Printed in the United States of America.

Cibula, Matt S.
    What's up with you, Taquandra Fu? / written by Matt Cibula ; illustrated by Brian Strassburg.
        p.   cm.
    Summary: Taquandra Fu, the weirdest girl in class, decides to try being normal for a change.
    ISBN 1-55933-212-3
    [1. Individuality—Fiction. 2. Humor stories. 3. Stories in rhyme.]   I. Strassburg, Brian John, ill.   II. Title
PZ8.3.C525Wh 1997
[Fic]—dc21   97-13617
                                                                                              CIP
                                                                                              AC

10 9 8 7 6 5 4 3 2 1
First Printing, December 1997

Meet Helga. She's a Skaddabinglehuznahaznahu. She's over 450 years old, which makes her just a youngster.

The Skaddabinglehuznahaznahu is a large, round, orange and yellow ungulate indigenous to Brazil, Tanzania, Micronesia, Timbuktu, Cucamonga, Shangri-La, Erehwon, Atlantis, your neighborhood, and other parts of the world where smart kids dwell. It is a gentle and noble beast, distinguished for its intelligence and playfulness, as well as several unusual physical characteristics:

Horns made of lip-smacking-good sugar candy, grown fresh every day

An accurate and complete map of the world on its torso, so it never gets lost

The ability to tap dance despite weighing over 1,000 pounds.

It also possesses an incredible aptitude for seeking fun in all its forms.

My name's Taquandra Fu and I'm the **weirDest** girl in class.

I have the kind of **weirDness** that nobody can surpass:

My boots are made of raisins and my hats are all stained glass,

And when it rains I wear an overcoat of shiny brass.

As you can tell, I'm strange indeed; I do things you don't do —

And everybody says, "What's up with you, Taquandra Fu?"

i say "**G**ood**b**ye" when I arrive and "**H**i" when I vamoo**s**e;

I ride the **SouL** **T**r**a**i**n** down to school (I ride on the caboose);

I eat a healthy lunch of **O**lives, hay, and **O**range juice;

I know my hair looks great because I used a little moo**s**e.

I tell a **m**illion **b**illion fibs, but all of them are true –

And everybody says, "What's up with you, **TaQuandra Fu?**"

I often say things sdrawkcab or I say them wrong side up.

I drink right off my plate and eat my pie right from my cup.

When I mean yes I shake my head; when I mean nope I yup.

I purrrrrr just like a pudding and meow just like a pup.

My favorite word is "Skaddabinglehuznahaznahu".

That's why I hear them say, "What's up with you, Taquandra Fu?"

The Skaddabingle

I have a friend who's Contrary, but I just call him Kid.
We go to the aquarium and hang out with the squid.
We know his name: it's Mr. Sloopus Alexander Pfhlydd;
He learned to siNG in London, but he grew up in Madrid.

daring herring

We're both quite odd and both quite proud of all our derring-do—
We laugh when people say, "What's up with you, TaQuandra Fu?"

SPAGHETTI DINNER
Friday Night
ST. PEGGY'S

But it's not always easy when you play the way I play.

I'm not as cool as Caroline or popular like Trey.

Last week I brought my special pumpkin-raspberry soufflé;

It came in thirty pieces and went home with me that way.

I wanted them to like it, but they all just said, "P.U.!

Please get it out of here! What's up with you, Taquandra Fu?"

I'm not exactly first one picked for any Kickball team.

Which sort of stinks, although it's not like kickball is my dream.

I ran for class vice-president and Jen said, "That's a Scream!"

I don't know what she meant, but it sure hurt my self-esteem.

Nobody's happy all the time, and sometimes I get blue—

Then I don't want to hear "What's up with you, TaQuandra Fu?"

I asked my mom if it was wrong that I am so biZarre.
Of course she said - 'cause she's a mom - "You're fine the way you are."
I asked my dad while he was busy practicing guitar;
He said to me, "Taquandra, you will always be my Star."

My parents think I'm perfect, which just means they have no clue
That anything is UP with me, their girl TaQuandra Fu.

So I made up my mind to be much closer to the norm.
And I took off my stained-glass hat (although it keeps me warm).
I got a hat like Caroline's to hide me from the storm
And changed my weirdo clothes and hair for styles more UNIFORM.

I told myself that being weird is something I outgrew.
I didn't want to hear "What's up with you, TaQuandra Fu?"

CAROLINE'S HAT

I took the bUs to school today. I did not board the train.
That hat like Caroline's was very good against the rain.
I kept all my unusual small thoughts inside my brain ← - - - - - - - - →
(And it was VERY difficult to stand up to the STRAIN).

But I am on a mission to be normal through and through
So nobody can say, "What's up with you, TaQuandra Fu?"

I got to school on time today - not early and not late.
I did just what the others did and did not deviate.
I ate whatever food it was they put upon my plate.
I did not zig. I did not zag. I only traveled STRAIGHT.

I kept my socks upon my feet and each one in its shoe -
And no one even asked, "What's up with you, Taquandra Fu?"

I guess my plan worked out 'cause Trey gave me his last balloon.

And Jen picked me at number three when we played ball at noon.

Then my best friend asked me to come and meet the new baboon.

I told him I was busy, but I felt real bad real soon

Because I watched him walk all by himself down to the zoo,

And I said to myself, "What's up with you, TaQuandra Fu?"

1 couldn't tell him why I'd changed my personality,
So I just sat there feeling smaller than the smallest flea.
What kind of person does Taquandra really want to be?
What good is being popular if I cannot be me?

small

smallest

I'd never really thought of this, so it was all brand-new –
It's kind of cool to hear "What's up with you, Taquandra Fu?"

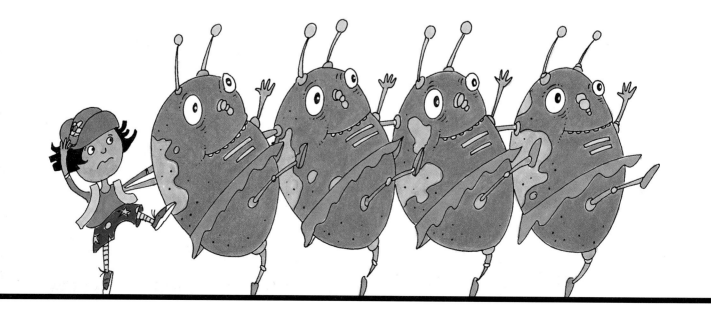

I thought about it and I thought a little while more;
My normal self and my wEirD self were in some kind of War.
Until we got to drama class. I played a dinosaur.

I l⊙⊙ked around and spoke my only line: a GIANT ...

OiNK

I got an "A" in Drama and my classmates said, "YahOOO! We're all so glad to have you back! Stay Weird, Taquandra Fu."

So that's the st⊙rY, reader, and there's not much more to tell.

At normalness I'm not so hot. At stRanGeneSs I excel.

That's why I ring bananas, and that's why I peel the b$e$ll.

And by the way, the new bab⊙⊙n can Y⊙Del really well.

OOOOOOO OODELE OOODELE DOOODLEEEE

Don't be surprised if one day I SuRf down your avenue —

And please call out to me, "What's up with you, TaQuandra Fu?"

YO..DEE.LA.Y...DE...HEE..HOO